Los Angeles

Published in the United States by

First Choice

P.O. Box 191126
San Diego, CA 92159

PHOTOGRAPHY / GREG LAWSON
RALPH CERNUDA PAGES 32, 54 & COVER
INTRODUCTION / TINA GOOLSBY
CAPTIONS / DAVID MICHAELS
TRANSLATIONS / GAVIN HYDE, MARIE-HELENE BUGNION
ROSELINDE KONRAD, KIMIE SMITH
TYPOGRAPHY / FRIEDRICH TYPOGRAPHY
PRINTED AND BOUND IN SINGAPORE BY IMAGO PRODUCTIONS

Our titles currently available or in production include: ARIZONA, CALIFORNIA, COLORADO,
HAWAII, LOS ANGELES, SAN DIEGO, SAN FRANCISCO, SANTA BARBARA, WESTERN OREGON.

The arrival of the first Yankee into the pueblo of Los Angeles reads today like a swash-buckling Hollywood Western. As the story goes, Joseph Chapman, member of a coast-raiding pirate band, was captured and taken in by Spanish Cavalry in 1818, becoming the area's first Anglo citizen in about 1821. Preceeding, and proceeding, Chapman are a cast of diverse characters who, over centuries, would be drawn to this unique coastal region of Southern California.

Over fifteen hundred years ago, Shoshone Indians arrived over Cajon Pass, establishing the brush-hut village of Yang-na. In 1769, Gaspar de Portola and his group of Spanish soldiers would overtake them, claiming the area for the Crown of Spain and founding a pueblo and a Franciscan mission, christened San Gabriel. The padres introduced the orange, the grape, long-horn cattle, and adobe brick architecture.

What drew these settlers to "El Pueblo de Nuestra Señora La Reina de Los Angeles," The Town of Our Lady of the Angels? Hearty soil, sunshine, three mountain ranges which buffer against extreme temperatures, and proximity to the Great Pacific were, and remain today, its natural enticements.

By 1784, retired Spanish soldiers were establishing a new aristocracy through government sponsored land grants. Half a century later, the Sonoran Mexicans staged a revolution, claiming ranchos for themselves and prospering on the lucrative hide-and-tallow trade. During the 1850s, however, Los Angeles rapidly transformed into a white man's domain, and cattle country became farm country. The arrival of the railroads, linking L.A. to San Francisco and coast to coast, resulted in the Great Real Estate Boom of 1887.

The genius and drive of certain remarkable men have made Los Angeles the core of economic, commercial, agricultural, and human resources of the West over the last century. In 1892, Ed Doheny tapped into an oil bonanza that would change the face and economy of the area in drastic ways. In 1899, Thomas Edison invented the "picture that moves," and right away, directors took the idea to the land of sunshine and varied terrain. The medium of film-making established Los Angeles, and especially Hollywood, as a cultural capital with worldwide impact. At the turn of the century, Henry Huntington's "red car" trolleys saw the mushrooming of numerous suburban towns along their tracks, and in 1913 William Mulholland's 240-mile aquaduct brought desperately needed water to them from Owens Valley.

Although the city proper covers only four hundred sixty-four square miles, the Greater L.A. area stretches inland to the San Bernardino Mountains and spills up and down the coast from Ventura to Orange County. This virtual city-state, united by a massive lacework of roads and freeways, nurtures an overwhelming abundance of wealth, glamour, culture, architecture, natural beauty, and ethnic diversity. Within Los Angeles proper are thirty-five museums, a hundred legitimate theatres, over sixty colleges and universities, miles of beachfront, and ethnic pockets scattered throughout.

From the eccentricity of Venice Beach to the ultimate glamour of Beverly Hills and the Miracle Mile, the Los Angeles area must be savored a bit at a time. Through these pages we could never attempt to capture the entire scope of today's Greater Los Angeles, but turn them slowly and experience a potpourri of its astounding character and richness.

La llegada del primer yanqui en el pueblo de Los Angeles parece hoy en día un cuento de hazañas del oeste primitivo, al estilo de Hollywood. Según el relato, Joseph Chapman, miembro de una cuadrilla de piratas que pillaban por la costa, fue capturado y sujetado por la caballería española en 1818, haciéndose el cautivo el primer ciudadano angloamericano alrededor de 1821. Precediendo a éste, y siguiéndole, encontramos un conjunto de actores quienes, sobre el curso de los siglos, sintieron la atracción de esta distintiva región costeña del sur de California.

Hace más de mil quinientos años, los indígenas del tribu Shoshone llegaron por el puerto serrano del Cajón, estableciendo la villa de Yang-na consistiendo en un grupo de chozas hechas del chaparral. En 1769, Gaspar de Portola y sus soldados españoles tomaron posesión de la zona en nombre de la Corona de España y establecieron un pueblo vinculado a una misión franciscana a la que dieron nombre de San Gabriel. Los padres introdujeron naranjos, viñas, ganado cuernilargo, y edificios de adobe.

¿Qué fue lo que atraía a éstos al "pueblo de Nuestra Señora la reina de Los Angeles"? Tierra buena, mucho sol, tres sierras que rechazaban temperaturas extremas, y la riqueza del gran Pacífico eran, y siguen siendo, sus gracias naturales.

Ya para 1784, algunos soldados españoles retirados iban formando una aristocracia por medio de grandes concesiones gubernamentales de tierras. Medio siglo después, los mexicanos de Sonora promovieron una revolución, reclamando los ranchos y prosperando con el comercio de pieles y sebo. Durante los años 1850-1860 sin embargo, Los Angeles se transformó de repente en un lugar bajo el dominio de intereses de los anglos, y las ganaderías se volvieron tierras de labranza. La llegada de los ferrocarriles, ligando a Los Angeles con San Francisco y atravesando el país entero, dieron el desarrollo decisivo para el *Great Real Estate Boom* (gran auge en valor de bienes raíces) de 1887.

La perspicacia y dinamismo de ciertos individuos han hecho de Los Angeles el centro de recursos económicos, comerciales, agrarios y humanos, en cuanto al Oeste, durante los últimos 100 años. En 1892, Ed Doheny taladró en un tesoro petrolero que cambiaría la fisonomía y la economía del área drásticamente. En 1899, Thomas Edison inventó la cinematografía y en seguida, los directores aplicaron la idea en esta región soleada con su terreno variado. El género de la cinematografía dió renombre a Los Angeles, y especialmente a Hollywood, como capital cultural con influencia mundial. Al iniciar el nuevo siglo, los tranvías de trole, denominados *red cars* (carros rojos), de Henry Huntington, vieron la expansión de numerosos pueblos suburbanos a lo largo de sus vías, y en 1913 el aqueducto de William Mulholland, contando 240 millas (380 kms) de largo, traía el agua que tanto les urgía, desde el valle de Owens.

Aunque la ciudad propia solamente ocupa cuatrocientos sesenta y cuatro millas cuadradas, la zona mayor de Los Angeles se extiende hacia el interior hasta la sierra de San Bernardino y se despliega del norte al sur entre Ventura y Orange County. Esta ciudad que importa como un estado, unida por una red formidable de autopistas, da lugar a una abundancia de caudal, encantamiento, cultura, arquitectura, belleza natural, y diversidad étnica. Dentro de la municipalidad propia de Los Angeles quedan treinta y cinco museos, un centenar de teatros legítimos con tablas, más de sesenta universidades, muchas millas de playa — y salpicados por todas partes, muchos barrios étnicamente variados.

Desde la eccentricidad de la playa de Venice hasta el embeleso impar de Beverly Hills y Miracle Mile ("la milla de milagros") Los Angeles se debe saborear poco a poco. En estas páginas nunca pudiéramos abrazar el rango entero de las delicias de la zona mayor, pero . . . hojee lentamente y conozca un popurrí de su carácter sorprendente y su riqueza asombrosa.

L'arrivée du premier homme blanc dans le village de Los Angeles se lit comme un western hollywoodien aventureux. Comme l'histoire nous l'indique, Joseph Chapman, membre d'une bande de pirates qui pillaient la côte, a été capturé et a dû s'engager dans la cavalerie espagnole en 1818. Vers 1821 il est devenu le premier citoyen Anglo-Saxon de la région. Avant et après Chapman, toute une troupe de personnages divers ont été attirés par cette magnifique région côtière de la Californie du Sud.

Il y a plus de mille cinq cents ans, des indiens Shoshone sont arrivés par le col de Cajon et ont établi le village de huttes de Yang-na. En 1769, Gaspar de Portola et sa troupe de soldats espagnols sont allés plus loin et ont réclamé ces territoires pour la couronne d'Espagne. Ils y ont fondé un village et une mission de Franciscains baptisée San Gabriel. Les moines y ont introduit l'orange, le raisin, la race des bovins à longues cornes et les habitations en tourbe.

Qu'est-ce qui attira ces colons à "El Pueblo de Nuestra Señora la Reina de Los Angeles", La Ville de Notre Dame la Reine des Anges? Un sol fertile, du soleil, trois chaînes de montagnes qui protègent la région contre des températures extrêmes et la proximité de l'océan pacifique faisaient, et font aujourd'hui, partie de ses attraits naturels.

En 1784 des soldats espagnols retraités formaient une nouvelle aristocratie grâce à des donations de terres du gouvernement. Un demi-siècle plus tard, les Mexicains de Sonora se sont révoltés et ont réclamés des ranchs pour eux et leurs familles. Ils ont prospéré grâce au commerce lucratif des sous-produits de l'élevage. Cependant, pendant les années 1850, Los Angeles s'est rapidement transformée en un domaine de l'homme blanc, et la terre d'élevage est devenue terre de cultures. L'arrivée des chemins de fer qui reliaient Los Angeles à San Francisco ainsi qu'une côte des Etats-Unis à l'autre produisit le grand boum immobilier de 1887.

Le génie et l'énergie de certains hommes remarquables ont fait de Los Angeles le centre économique, commercial, agriculturel et social de l'Ouest des Etats-Unis pendant le siècle dernier. En 1892, Ed Doheny y a découvert et exploité un large gisement de pétrole, ce qui a changé l'aspect et l'économie de la région de façon radicale. En 1899, Thomas Edison a inventé "la photo qui bouge", et, immédiatement, des metteurs en scène s'emparèrent de l'idée pour l'implanter dans ce pays de soleil au terrain varié. L'activité cinématographique a fait de Los Angeles, et spécialement d'Hollywood, la capitale mondiale du cinéma. Au début du siècle, les tramways "wagon rouge" d'Henry Huntington ont vu le bourgeonnement de nombreuses villes de banlieue le long de leur itinéraire, et, en 1913, l'aqueduc long de deux cent quarante miles (380 kilomètres) de William Mulholland leur a apporté l'eau dont elles avaient un besoin urgent de la vallée Owens.

Bien que la cité elle-même ne couvre que quatre cent soixante-quatre miles, la région plus vaste de Los Angeles s'étend à l'intérieur jusqu'aux montagnes San Bernardino et le long de la côte de Ventura à Orange County. Cette ville-état, unie par un réseau impressionnant de routes et d'autoroutes, nourrit une abondance incroyable de richesse, d'élégance, culture, d'architecture, de beauté naturelle et de diversité ethnique. Los Angeles proprement dit abrite trente-cinq musées, cent théâtres, plus de soixante collèges et universités, des kilomètres de plage et diverses communautés ethniques.

De l'excentricité de Venice Beach à l'élégance sophistiquée de Beverly Hills et du Miracle Mile, la région de Los Angeles doit être savourée petit à petit. A travers ces quelques pages nous ne pourrions jamais saisir toute l'importance du Los Angeles d'aujourd'hui, mais, lecteurs, tournez-les lentement et vous goûterez un potpourri de sa personnalité étonnante et de sa richesse.

Der Bericht vom Erscheinen des ersten Yankees im Pueblo Los Angeles hört sich heute an wie ein waschechter Western aus Hollywood. Laut Überlieferung war ein gewisser Joseph Chapman, Mitglied einer an der Küste plündernden Piratenbande, gefangen- und dann 1818 von der spanischen Kavallerie aufgenommen worden, und etwa 1821 wurde er in dieser Gegend der erste Staatsbürger englischer Abstammung. Während der folgenden Jahrhunderte sollte dieses einzigartige südkalifornische Küstengebiet die unterschiedlichsten Menschentypen anziehen.

Vor über fünfzehnhundert Jahren kamen die Shoshone-Indianer über den Cajon-Paß in dieses Gebiet, und es entstand die Hüttensiedlung Yang-na. Im Jahre 1769 wurden sie von Gaspar de Portola und seinem Trupp spanischer Soldaten überrannt, die das Gebiet für die spanische Krone in Anspruch nahmen und ein Pueblo mit einer Franziskanermission gründeten, das sie San Gabriel nannten. Die Pater führten Apfelsinen, Trauben, langhörniges Vieh und Adobeziegelbau ein.

Was zog denn nun diese Siedler ins „Pueblo de Nuestra Señora La Reina de Los Angeles", in die „Stadt der Himmelskönigin der Engel"? Der Grund dieser Anziehungskraft war und ist noch heute der Grund und Boden, der Sonnenschein, drei Gebirgsketten, die Schutz bieten gegen extreme Temperaturen, und die Nähe des Stillen Ozeans.

Spanische Soldaten mit beendeter Dienstzeit bildeten seit 1784 durch ihren (ihnen vom Staat übertragenen) Landbesitz eine neue Oberschicht. Ein halbes Jahrhundert später rebellierten die Mexikaner dieser Gegend, beanspruchten selbst den Besitz von Ranchos und wurden durch den einträglichen Fell- und Talghandel wohlhabend. Während der fünfziger Jahre des neunzehnten Jahrhunderts wandelte sich Los Angeles jedoch schnell zur Domäne der Weißen, und Weideland wurde zu Ackerland. Durch den Bau von Eisenbahnstrecken, die L.A. mit San Francisco, und Ost- und Westküste miteinander verbanden, kam es 1887 zu einem gewaltigen Aufschwung im Landbesitz, dem „Great Real Estate Boom".

Einige hervorragende Persönlichkeiten haben mit ihrem Weitblick und ihrer Schaffenskraft Los Angeles im Laufe des vorigen Jahrhunderts zum Ausgangspunkt wirtschaftlicher und geistiger Initiative gemacht. Ed Doheny, zum Beispiel, brachte 1892 durch seine Ölentdeckung eine Entwicklung ins Rollen, die Gestalt und Wirtschaft des ganzen Gebietes drastisch verändern sollte. 1899 erfand Thomas Edison das „bewegliche Bild", und sofort machten sich die Filmregisseure auf ins Land der Sonne und der vielfältigen Landschaft. Durch das Filmschaffen etablierte sich Los Angeles, und besonders Hollywood, als Kulturzentrum von weltweiter Bedeutung. Um die Jahrhundertwende sprangen auf der Straßenbahnstrecke von Henry Huntingtons „roten Wagen" zahlreiche Vororte aus dem Boden, und das dringend nötige Wasser brachte ihnen 1913 William Mulhollands 380 Kilometer langer Aquadukt.

Obwohl die Stadt selbst nur 1200 Quadratkilometer umfaßt, erstreckt sich das Gesamtgebiet, das die Vororte mit einschließt, bis an die San Bernardino-Berge und zieht sich verstreut von Ventura bis Orange County nördlich und südlich die Küste entlang. Diese Stadt, die schon mehr ein „Staat" ist, der durch ein ausgedehntes Netz von Straßen und Autobahnen zusammengehalten wird, ist die Basis einer geradezu überwältigenden Fülle von Wohlstand, Luxus, von Kulturellem, von Baustilen und landschaftlicher Schönheit, von völkischer Vielfalt. Innerhalb des engeren Stadtbereichs von Los Angeles gibt es fünfunddreißig Museen, hundert Schauspielhäuser, über sechzig College und Universitäten, kilometerlange Strände und, überall verstreut, Inseln diverser Volksgruppen.

Ob es sich nun um die Ausgefallenheit eines Ortes wie Venice Beach handelt oder um den äußersten Glanz und Luxus von Beverly Hills und der „Miracle Mile", Groß-Los Angeles muß man stückchenweise genießen. Das gesamte Gebiet kann in seinem Ausmaß auf den folgenden Seiten nicht eingefangen werden, aber ein aufmerksames Betrachten öffnet den Blick auf eine erstaunliche Vielfalt im Wesen der Stadt und ihrer Menschen.

ヤンキー第一号のロサンゼルス村入りの話は、今日では、まるで硝煙のうずまくハリウッド製の西部劇そのものといった観があります。いい伝えによれば、1818年、当時西海岸一帯をあらしまわっていた海賊の一人ジョセフ・チャップマンがスペインの騎兵隊に捕えられ、1821年頃ロサンゼルスにつれてこられました。これが、アングロサクソン系市民がこの地方に到着した最初の出来事だったそうです。このチャップマンに先だつこと何世紀も前に、又彼の後も引き続き数多くの性格をことにした人々が、際立った特徴をもつ南カルフォルニア沿岸地方にひきつけられてやってきました。

今から1500年以上も昔には、ショショーン・インディアンが今日のカホン峠にたどりつき、ヤングナと呼ばれた部落を形成しました。1769年になると、スペイン人がスパル・デ・ポルトラと彼の兵士等がこれらのインディアンを征服しました。そして辺り一帯をスペイン王の領土とし、フランシスコ会系の教会、ミッション・サン・ガブリエルを建立しました。ミッションの僧侶達はオレンヂ、ぶどう、家畜、アドベとよばれる日干しれんがの建築方法を導入しました。

今日ロサンゼルスとよばれているこの土地、スペイン語では「天使の聖母の村」という意味の「エル・プエブロ・デ・ヌヱヌトラ・セニョーラ・ラ・レイナ・デ・ロス・アンヘレス」がこれらの人々を引きつけた魅力は何だったのでしょう。肥沃な土地、太陽の光、寒暑の着をおさえる役目を果す三つの山脈、そして大平洋への容易なる接近は、当地も今も多くの人々の心を魅了してしまいます。

1784年までは、引退したスペイン人兵士達が本国政府より譲渡された土地を元に、新興貴族階級を形成していました。ところがその半世紀後には、今日のメキシコ北部のシナロアに住むメキシコ人達が革命をおこし、拡大した面積の牧場のほとんどが彼等によっておさえられてしまいました。この新しい地主達は生皮と獣脂の商売に成功し、大いに繁栄をほこりました。しかし1850年代になると、ロサンゼルスは急速に白人の領域となり、牧場の多くは農場にかわってゆきました。そして、ロサンゼルスとサンフランシスコ、やがて東海岸を結ぶ鉄道の設置は、1887年の不動産ブームをひきおこしたのです。

何人かの才覚ある人々の才能と行動力は過去一世紀の間に、ロサンゼルスを西海岸における経済、商業、農業、有能な人材の集まる中心地へと仕上げてゆきました。1892年のエド・ドヒィーニーの油田開発成功は辺りの経済と様子をすっかり一変してしまいました。1899年にはトマス・エジソンが「動く絵」を発明し、映画監督達はすぐさまそれを太陽と変化に豊む土地にもちこんで来ました。映画製作はロサンゼルスを、特にハリウッドを世界的影響力を持つ一つの文化的中心地にしてしまいました。今世紀初頭になると、ヘンリー・ハンティングトンの赤い路面電車が出現し、その沿線に数多くの効外住宅が作られました。そして長らく渇望されていた水道がウィリアム・マルホランドによってオーエン渓谷よりひき入れられました。全長240マイル、1913年のことでした。

ロサンゼルス市そのものゝ面積はほんの464平方マイルにすぎませんが、それをとり囲む大ロサンゼルス都市圏となると、内陸部はサン・ベルナルディーノ山脈、沿岸部は北のヴェントゥーラ郡から南のオレンヂ郡へと拡大に広がっています。このそれ自体州ともいえる大きな面積を網目のように広がった高速道路、支線道路によって連がれ、想像を絶する富、華麗、文化、建築、自然美、そして多様な人種を宿しています。ロサンゼルス本市内には35の博物、美術館、1000の劇場、60余りの二年制、四年制の大学、何マイルにも及ぶ海岸、そして様々の人種の共同体が点在しています。

奇をてらったヴェニス・ビーチの風俗から豪華けんらんたるビバリー・ヒルズと近くの高価な商品の並ぶミラクル・マイルズの商店街と、ロサンゼルスの風味は少しずつ吟味されなければなりません。以下の頁だけから今日の大ロサンゼルス都市圏の全像を握むことは難しいのですが、どうぞゆっくり頁をくりながら、その驚嘆すべき性格と豊かさを経験なさって下さい。

Los Angeles

The First Interstate Bank Building, tallest building in Los Angeles, and downtown architecture contrast (left) with historic Olvera Street.

El First Interstate Bank Building, el edificio más alto de la ciudad de Los Angeles, y otras edificaciones arquitectónicas situadas en el centro de la ciudad contrastan (izquierda) con la histórica Olvera Street.

Le bâtiment de la banque First Interstate, le plus haut de Los Angeles, et l'architecture du centre ville contraste avec la rue historique Olvera Street (à gauche).

First Interstate Bank Building, das höchste Gebäude in Los Angeles, und andere Gebäude im Stadtzentrum, die (links) einen schönen Kontrast zur historischen Olivera Street bilden.

由緒あるオルベラ・ストリートと対照的な、ロサンゼルスーの高層ビル、ザ・ファースト・インターステート・バンク・ビル及びその他のダウンタウンの建築物（左）。

Little Tokyo's New Otani Complex. (left) The restored "Angels Flight."

El nuevo Otani Complex (Complejo Otani) de Little Tokio (El Pequeño Tokio). (izquierda) El recién restaurado "Angels Flight" (Vuelo de Angeles)

Le nouveau complexe Otani de Little Tokyo. Le « Angels Flight » restauré (à gauche).

New Otani-Komplex in Little Tokyo. (links) Das restaurierte "Angels Flight".

リトル・トーキョーのニュー・オータニ・コンプレックス。（左）修復された「エンジェルズ・フライト」。

Speeding art lovers can only glimpse their favorite works in the city's new 'freeway galleries'.

Muy al galope goza el aficionado las nuevas 'galerías de autopista'.

Les amoureux des visites artistiques rapides pourront seulement jeter un coup d'œil sur leurs œuvres préférées de long des nouvelles "galeries sur autoroute" le la cité.

In den neuen „Autobahn-Galerien" muß sich der vorbeibrausende Kunstliebhaber mit einem kurzen Blick auf sein Lieblingswerk begnügen.

ロサンゼルスの新名所「高速道路ギャラリー」も一瞬のうちにすぎさってしまいます。

From its home base in Carson, the airship Columbia is seen aloft throughout the Southland.

Desde su base en Carson el dirigible *Columbia* se presenta por todos los horizontes del sur del estado.

De sa base à Carson, on peut voir le dirigeable *Columbia* flotter dans les cieux de Californie du sud.

Von seinem Heimathafen in Carson aus ist das Luftschiff *Columbia* überall im *Southland* am Himmel zu sehen.

地元カーソン市上空に浮ぶ飛行船コロンビア号。

MacArthur Park and skyscrapers in downtown.
(right) Wilshire Boulevard's "Queen of Angels."

El MacArthur Park y los rascacielos del centro de la ciudad.
(derecha) La "Queen of Angels" (Reina de Angeles) de
Wilshire Boulevard.

Le parc MacArthur et les gratte-ciel du centre ville.
« Queen of Angels » sur le boulevard Wilshire (à droite).

MacArthur-Park und Wolkenkratzer im Stadtzentrum.
(rechts) "Queen of Angels" auf dem Wilshire Boulevard.

ダウンタウンの摩天楼とマッカサー公園。（右）
ウイルシャー・ブルバードの「クイーン・オブ・エンジェルズ」。

Included in downtown's futuristic architecture are the looming Bonaventure Hotel and (right) the Crocker Center towers which seem, at times, to mingle with the clouds.

Elementos de la arquitectura futurística del centro son el imponente *Bonaventure Hotel* y (dcha.) las torres del *Crocker Center* que a veces parecen unirse con las nubes.

Parmi les modèles d'architecture futuriste du centre-ville on peut distinguer l'imposant hôtel *Bonaventure* et (à droite) les tours du centre *Crocker* qui, par instants, se perdent dans les nuages.

Beispiele des futuristischen Baustils der Innenstadt sind die riesigen Wolkenkratzer des *Bonaventure*-Hotels und (rechts) des *Crocker Centers*, die manchmal in den Wolken zu verschwinden scheinen.

雲とたわむれる未来派のビル、ボナベニチャー・ホテルと、（右）　クロッカー・センター・タワー。

Luminescent streaks on the Harbor Freeway. (left) Lofty Griffith Park Observatory. (overleaf) The sleeping giant tucked in by a midnight sea and the San Gabriel Mountains.

Rayos fosforescentes sobre el *Harbor Freeway*. (izqda.) El observatorio celestial de *Griffith Park*. (pag. sig.) El ángel gigante acostado entre el mar nocturno y la sierra de *San Gabriel*.

Traînées lumineuses sur l'autoroute *Harbor*. (à gauche) L'observatoire élevé du parc *Griffith*. (au verso) La cité endormie entre l'océan et les montagnes *San Gabriel*.

Bunte Lichtstreifen auf dem *Harbor Freeway*. (links) Die hochgelegene Sternwarte in *Griffith Park*. (umseitig) Die Stadt, ein schlafender Riese, eingehüllt ins nächtliche Meer und die *San Gabriel*-Berge.

ハーバー高速道路の光の流れ。（左）　グリフィス天文台。（離面）　夜のしじまに囲まれて。マウント・ウィルソンより望む。

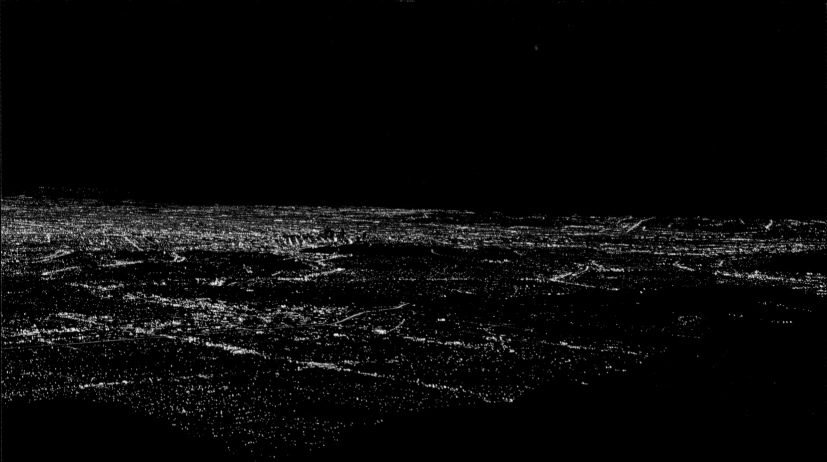

Queen Mary in Long Beach and (left) an example of the street lamps that still grace Los Angeles streets.

El Queen Mary, en Long Beach y (izquierda) un ejemplo de los faroles que aún adornan las calles de Los Angeles.

Le Queen Mary à Long Beach et (à gauche) un exemple des lampadaires qui ornent toujours les rues de Los Angeles.

Queen Mary in Long Beach und (links) ein Exemplar der Straßenlaternen, die immer noch die Straßen von Los Angeles zieren.

ロング・ビーチのクイーン・メアリーと（左）ロサンゼルスの街路を今だに優雅に彩る街灯の例。

The World Trade Center Building, Long Beach, reflected from the ARCO Center.
(right) A silhouette of the Vincent Thomas Bridge.

El World Trade Center Building, en Long Beach, reflejado desde el Arco Center. (derecha)
Una silueta del Vincent Thomas Bridge.

Le bâtiment du World Trade Center de Long Beach reflété par le centre ARCO. La silhouette
du pont Vincent Thomas se découpe à droite.

Das Gebäude des World Trade Center, Long Beach, wie es sich im AROO Center
widerspiegelt. (rechts) Eine Silhouette der Vincent Thomas Bridge.

アルコ・センターからロングビーチに移転したワールド・トレード・センター・ビル。（右）
ビンセント・トーマス・ブリッジのシルエット。

UCLA and surrounding Westwood. (right) A sculpture at the Huntington Library.

La UCLA y Westwood, a sus alrededores. (derecha) Una escultura en la Huntington Library.

UCLA et le voisinage de Westwood. Une sculpture de la bibliothèque de Huntington (à droite).

UCLA und das angrenzende Westwood. (rechts) Eine Skulptur in der Huntington Library.

UCLA（カリフォルニア州立大学ロサンゼルス校）と周辺のウエストウッド地区。（右）ハンティントン図書館の彫刻。

Sun seekers at Aliso Beach. (left) Dana Point Harbor, Dana Point.

Aficionados del sol en la playa de *Aliso*. (izqda.) Puerto de *Dana Point*.

Les adorateurs du soleil sur la plage d'*Aliso*. (à gauche) La crique de *Dana Point*, Dana Point.

Sonnenliebhaber am Strand von *Aliso Beach*. (links) Der Hafen von *Dana Point*.

アリソ・ビーチ。 （左） ダナ岬ハーバー。

Crescent Bay Beach, Laguna Hills, along the scenic Orange County coast.

La playa de *Crescent Bay, Laguna Hills*, por la costa vistosa de *Orange County*.

La plage de *Crescent Bay*, à *Laguna Hills*, le long de la côte d'*Orange County*, côte qui offre des vues splendides.

Der Strand von *Crescent Bay* in *Laguna Hills* an der malerischen Küste von *Orange County*.

風光明美で知られるオレンヂ郡の沿岸ラグナ・ヒルズにある三日月湾海岸。
クレセント・ベイ・ビーチ

A Palos Verdes Peninsula seascape and (right) Point Vicente Lighthouse.

Hermosa vista del mar en la península de *Palos Verdes* y (dcha.) faro de *Point Vicente*.

Paysage de la péninsule de *Palos Verdes* et (à droite) le phare *Point Vicente*.

Seelandschaft der Halbinsel *Palos Verdes* und (rechts) der Leuchtturm von *Point Vicente*.

パロス・ヴェルデス半島と、（右）　ヴィセンテ岬の燈台。

With daylight spent a windsurfer stays his sport until another day.

Llegado el crepúsculo, este surfeador de vela suspende su deporte hasta el día siguiente.

La lumière du jour disparaît; un véliplanchiste remet son expédition à un autre jour.

Der Sport geht morgen weiter: im ausgehenden Tageslicht packt ein Windsurfer ein.

又のウインドサーフィンを楽しみに。

Along the 'Grand Canal' of Balboa Island, one of Newport Bay's aquatic communities.

A lo largo del *Grand Canal* de la isla de *Balboa*, uno de los barrios acuáticos de *Newport Bay*.

Le long du *Grand Canal* de *Balboa Island*, l'un des centres nautiques de *Newport Bay*.

Am *Grand Canal* von *Balboa Island*, einem der typischen Badeorte von *Newport Bay*.

水郷ニューポート湾の一角、バルボアアイランドのグランド・カナルにて。

Downtown Santa Monica structures facing Palisades Park and the blue Pacific.

Edificios del centro de Santa Mónica frente al parque *Palisades* y el azulado Pacífico.

Les bâtiments du centre-ville à *Santa Monica* font face au parc *Palisades* et à l'océan pacifique.

Diese Gebäude in der Innenstadt von *Santa Monica* haben Blickrichtung auf den *Palisades*-Park und den blauen Pazifik.

サンタ・モニカの下町と、太平洋を脊にしたパリセード公園。

The old Fox tower still rises on the Westwood Village Theatre, backdropped by UCLA campus buildings, Westwood.

La vieja torre del *Fox* aun se alza sobre el *Westwood Village Theatre*; y en el fondo los edificios del campus de *UCLA* (la Universidad de California), *Westwood*.

L'ancienne tour *Fox* s'élève toujour au-dessus du cinéma *Westwood Village Theatre*; à l'arrière-plan on aperçoit les bâtiments du campus de l'université *UCLA* à *Westwood*.

Der alte *Fox*-Bau ist immer noch da im *Westwood Village Theatre*-Komplex, mit den Campusgebäuden von *UCLA* in *Westwood* als Hintergrund.

その昔の二十世紀フォックス社の塔はまだウエストウッド、ヴィレッヂ劇場の上にそびえています。背景はUCLAのキャンパスと校舎。ウエストウッド。

West Hollywood's streamlined Pacific Design Center caters to the interior design trade.

El modernísimo *Pacific Design Center* de West Hollywood se dedica a la industria de la decoración de interiores.

Le *Pacific Design Center* de West Hollywood sert les intérêts des architectes d'intérieur.

Das elegante *Pacific Design Center* in West Hollywood ist auf Innendekoration spezialisiert.

流線形の建物パシフィック・デザイン・センターは室内装飾を手がけています。ウエスト・ハリウッド。

A palm lined residential street in Beverly Hills and (right) Century Plaza Towers in ultra-modern Century City.

Una calle residencial luciendo filas de palmeras en *Beverly Hills* y (dcha.) *Century Plaza Towers* en el complejo ultra-moderno, *Century City*.

Une rue résidentielle de *Beverly Hills* bordée de palmiers et (á droite) les tours du *Century Plaza* qui font partie du centre commercial ultra-moderne *Century City*.

Eine mit Palmen bestandene Straße in einer Wohngegend von *Beverly Hills* und (rechts) *Century Plaza Towers* im hochmodernen *Century City*.

ヤシの並木に飾られたビバリー・ヒルズの住宅街と（右）　超近代的なセンチュリー・シティーのセンチュリー・プラザ・タワーズ。

Shopping for art at a Beverly Hills art show in Beverly Garden Park and (left) a park fountain.

De compras entre obras de arte en una exposición de *Beverly Hills*, en *Beverly Garden Park* y (izqda.) una fuente del parque.

Acheteurs de tableaux à une exposition de *Beverly Hills* au parc *Beverly Garden* et (à gauche) une fontaine du parc.

Beim Einkauf auf einer Kunstausstellung im *Beverly Garden*-Park in *Beverly Hills* und (links) ein Brunnen im Park.

アート・ショー。（左）　噴水。ビバリー・ガーデン公園にて。

A free to the public concert in Beverly Hills. (right) The Mark Taper Forum, just one section of The Music Center, L.A.'s expansive downtown entertainment complex.

Un concierto de entrada gratis en *Beverly Hills*. (dcha.) El *Mark Taper Forum*, solo una parte del *Music Center*, la expansiva instalación del centro dedicada a los espectáculos.

Un concert gratuit à *Beverly Hills*. (à droite) Le *Mark Taper Forum* représente seulement une des sections du centre culturel *The Music Center*, ensemble culturel le plus vaste du centre de *Los Angeles*.

Ein eintrittsfreies Konzert in *Beverly Hills*. (rechts) Das *Mark Taper Forum*, nur ein Teil des *Music Centers*, des großzügigen Kunst- und Unterhaltungszentrums in der Innenstadt von *Los Angeles*.

ビバリー・ヒルズの無料音楽会。（右）　マーク・テーパー・フォラムは拡張を続けるロサンゼル市下町の娯楽街ミュージック・センターの一角にあります。

A Wilshire District profile from the Hollywood Hills. (left) Farmers Market, a fine food bazaar.

Un perfil del distrito de *Wilshire* desde *Hollywood Hills*. (izqda.) *Farmers' Market* (el 'mercado de los campesinos'), venta de productos buenos y frescos.

Wilshire District, vu des collines d'*Hollywood*. (à gauche) *Farmers Market*, un marché.

Blick auf den Stadtteil *Wilshire* vom höhergelegenen *Hollywood* aus. (links) *Farmers Market*, eine gute Einkaufsgelegenheit für Lebensmittel.

ハリウッド・ヒルズからみたウイルシャー地区。 （左） ファーマーズ・マーケットには飲食店が軒を連ねています。

The beautiful Los Angeles County Museum of Natural History in Exposition Park.

El hernoso *Museum of Natural History* (museo de ciencias naturales) del condado de *Los Angeles en Exposition Park*.

Le magnifique musée d'histoire naturelle de *Los Angeles County* au parc *Exposition*.

*Das sch*öne naturkundliche *Los Angeles County*-Museum im *Exposition*-Park.

万博公園にあるロサンゼル自然歴史博物館。

USC campus structures from the rose garden in Exposition Park.

Edificios de la *University of Southern California (USC)* vistos desde el jardín de rosales en *Exposition Park*.

Les bâtiments du campus de l'université *USC*, vus du jardin des roses au parc *Exposition*.

Die Gebäude des *USC*-Campus vom Rosengarten im *Exposition Park* aus gesehen.

万博公園のバラ園より望む南カルフォルニア大学。

A small segment of Chinatown, the mid-city cultural center of Southland Chinese.

Un trozo de *Chinatown* ('barrio de los chinos') centro cultural de los chinos residentes del sur de California.

Une partie de *Chinatown*, le centre culturel des Chinois de Californie du Sud, situé au centre de la ville.

Ein Stückchen *Chinatown*, dem Kulturzentrum der *Southland*-Chinesen in Stadtmitte.

チャイナ・タウンにて。

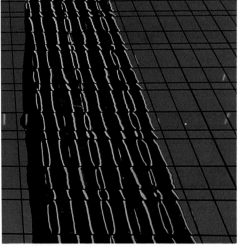

Downtown architectural contrasts and (right) William Mulholland Memorial Fountain, Griffith Park.

Contrastes arquitectónicos del centro y (dcha.) Memorial Fountain (fuente) de *William Mulholland, Griffith Park*.

Contrastes d'architecture du centre-ville et (à droite) la fontaine à la mémoire de *William Mulholland,* au parc *Griffith.*

*Bauliche Gegens*ätze in der Innenstadt und (rechts) der Gedenkbrunnen für *William Mulholland* im *Griffith Park*.

変化に豊む下町の建物。（右）　グリフィス公園内のウィリアム・マルホランド記念噴水。

The Hollywood sign on Mt. Lee looks down on 'The Bowl', Hollywood's distinctive outdoor amphitheater.

El letrero de Hollywood que lleva *Mt. Lee* domina al *Bowl*, su distintivo anfíteatro al aire libre.

Le logo d'Hollywood sur *Mt. Lee* surplombe *The Bowl*, l'amphithéâtre extérieur le plus connu d'Hollywood.

Die Beschriftung „Hollywood" auf *Mt. Lee* bildet den Hintergrund zu *The Bowl*, dem berühmten Freilichttheater in Hollywood.

マウント・リー山上のハリウッドのサインが見下す屋外円形劇場、ハリウッド・ボール。

Hollywood's familiar skyline and (right) Mann's Chinese Theatre.

El horizonte familiar de *Hollywood* y (dcha.) *Mann's Chinese Theatre*.

La silhouette familière des gratte-ciels d'*Hollywood* et (à droite) *Mann's Chinese Theatre*.

Das bekannte Panorama von *Hollywood* und (rechts) *Mann's Chinese Theatre*.

ハリウッドおなじみのスカイライン。(右) マンズ・チャイニーズ・シアター。

From Mulholland Drive the views are fantastic day or night of the sprawling San Fernando Valley and the mountainous walls that contain it.

Desde *Mulholland Drive* las vistas del valle de *San Fernando* y sus murallas montañosas siempre son fantásticas, sea de día o de noche.

De *Mulholland Drive* la vue est fantastique, de jour comme de nuit, sur la vallée *San Fernando*, délimitée par les parois des montagnes.

Bei Tag und bei Nacht bietet *Mulholland Drive* wunderschöne Ausblicke auf das ausgedehnte Tal *San Fernando Valley* und auf die Bergzüge, die es einschließen.

マルホランド・ドライブより眺めるサン・フェルナンド・バリーの景色は昼夜をとわず見事です。

The Tournament of Roses Parade, Norton Simon Museum and (right) City Hall, Pasadena.

La procesión del Tourneo de Rosas, el *Norton Simon Museum,* y (dcha.) City Hall (la Alcadía), Pasadena.

Le défilé du *Tournament of Roses,* le musée *Norton Simon* et (à droite) la marie à Pasadena.

Der Festzug anläßlich des *Tournament of Roses,* das *Norton Simon*-Museum und (rechts) das Rathaus in Pasadena.

パサデナの名物ローズ・パレードと、ノートン・サイモン美術館。

Queen Anne Cottage and a peacock on the grounds at Los Angeles State and County Arboretum, Arcadia.

Queen Anne Cottage y un pavo real en el recinto del criadero de árboles, *Los Angeles State and County Arboretum*, Arcadia.

Le *Queen Anne Cottage* et un paon sur les pelouses du *Los Angeles State and County Arboretum* à Arcadia.

Die *Queen Anne Cottage* und ein Fasan im Park des *Los Angeles State and County Arboretum* in Arcadia.

クィーン・アン時代風の建物とクジャク。アル
カディアのロサンゼルス州郡立植物園にて。

City Walks at Universal Studios and the world-famous Hard Rock Cafe.

City Walks (Paseos de la ciudad) y el Hard Rock Cafe, en Universal Studios.

City Walks et le Hard Rock Café aux Universal Studios.

City Walks und Hard Rock Cafe in den Universal Studios.

ユニバーサル・スタジオのハードロック・カフェとシティ・ウォークス。

Minutes from town are all season Lake Arrowhead and (right) Big Bear Lake.

A un paso están estas lagunas aptas para recreo en todas las estaciones, *Lake Arrowhead* y (dcha.) *Big Bear Lake*.

A quelques minutes de la ville se trouvent les lacs jamais asséchés *Lake Arrowhead* et (à droite) *Big Bear Lake*.

Nur wenige Minuten von der Stadt entfernt und in jeder Jahreszeit zugänglich sind die Seen *Lake Arrowhead* und (rechts) *Big Bear Lake*.

四季を通じて楽しめるアローヘッド・レークと、ビッグ・ベア・レークも町から遠くありません。

(Preceeding) Rim of the World Drive provides spectacular San Bernardino Mountain vistas. Shown above are crashing waves along the Ventura County coastline.

(pag. ant.) *Rim of the World Drive* (paseo del canto del mundo) ofrece vistas panorámicas de la sierra de *San Bernardino*. Aquí brincan las olas de la costa del condado de Ventura.

(photo précédente) La route *Rim of the World Drive* offre une vue exceptionelle des montagnes *San Bernardino*. Ci-dessus, des vagues qui se brisent le long de la côte de *Ventura County*.

(Vorhergehend) Die Straße *Rim of the World Drive* bietet fabelhafte Ausblicke auf die *San Bernardino Mountains*. (Oben) Wellen brechen sich an der Küste von *Ventura County*.

（前 2 ページ）　世界の縁と名ずけられたリム・オブ・ザ・ワールド・ドライブは、サン・ベルナルディーノ山の壮観な景色を味あわせてくれます。（上）　ヴェントゥーラ郡沿岸を洗う白波。

Peaceful grasslands of inland Ventura County near Ojai.

Pastos bucólicos del interior del condado de *Ventura* cerca de Ojai.

Prairies paisibles de l'intérieur à *Ventura County* près d'Ojai.

Friedliches Weideland im Innern von *Ventura County* bei Ojai.

のどかな内陸部の草原。ヴェントゥーラ郡オーハイの近くにて。

A beach party at Leo Carrillo State Beach.   (right) Reflections at day's end in Point Mugu State Park.

Fiesta en la playa estatal de *Leo Carrillo*.   (dcha.) Reflejos del crepúsculo en el parque estatal *Point Mugú*.

Un pique-nique sur la plage à *Leo Carrillo State Beach*.   (à droite) Reflets du couchant dans le parc de *Point Mugu State Park*.

Strandleben im Strandpark *Leo Carrillo*.   (rechts) Spiegelbilder gegen Abend im Park von *Point Mugu*.

ビーテ・パーティー。レオ・カリリョ州立海岸。（右）　ムグ岬州立公園の夕景色。

Homes above Carbon Canyon near Malibu view both the mountains and the sea.

Hogares en lo alto de *Carbon Canyon* cerca de *Malibu* tienen ambas vistas del mar y de las montañas.

Les maisons au-dessus du *Carbon Canyon* près de *Malibu* ont vue sur les montagnes et sur l'ocean.

Die Wohnhäuser an den Hängen des *Carbon Canyon* bei *Malibu* überblicken die Berge wie auch das Meer.

海と山の景色を楽む。マリブ海岸近くのカーボン・キャニオンにて。

A unique home nestled in the panoramic Santa Monica Mountains.

Un distintivo hogar anidado en las montañas panorámicas de
Santa Mónica.

Une maison originale nichée dans les montagnes panoramiques de
Santa Monica.

Ein höchst individuelles Haus, „eingebettet" im weiten Bergland, den
Santa Monica Mountains.

サンタ・モニカ山脈の家々。

Catching a wave at famous Malibu Surfrider State Beach.

Tomando una ola en la famosa playa estatal *Malibu Surfrider*.

Un surfer prend une vague sur la célèbre plage de *Malibu Surfrider State Beach*.

Im Wettkampf mit den Wellen am berühmten *Malibu Surfrider*-Strandpark.

マリブ・サーフライダー州立海岸にて。

Picturesque Malibu Pier, built near the turn of the century and rebuilt once since then.

El muelle pintoresco *Malibu Pier*, construido al principio del siglo y después renovado.

La jetée pittoresque de *Malibu Pier*, construite au début du siècle et reconstruite depuis.

Der malerische *Malibu Pier*, der um die Jahrhundertwende erbaut und seither neuerrichtet wurde.

今世紀初頭に建てられ、後再建されたマリブさん橋。

Two views of Marina del Rey, which harbors over 10,000 small craft.

Dos vistas de *Marina del Rey*, la que da puerto seguro a más de 10,000 barcos de tamaño menor.

Deux vues de *Marina del Rey*, port qui abrite plus de 10,000 petits bateaux de plaisance.

Zwei Ansichten von *Marina del Rey*, wo über 10 000 Boote im Hafen Platz finden.

1万隻以上の小型船を収容するマリナ・デル・レイのヨットハーバー。

The Los Angeles skyline at dusk and (right) theme building at Los Angeles International Airport.

El horizonte de Los Angeles entre dos luces y (dcha.) el sugestivo *theme building* ('edificio del tema') en el Aeropuerto Internacional de Los Angeles.

Silhouettes des gratte-ciels de Los Angeles au crépuscule et (à droite) un bâtiment à forme originale de l'aéroport international de Los Angeles.

Das Panorama von Los Angeles in der Abenddämmerung und (rechts) das Wahrzeichen von Los Angeles am Internationalen Flughafen.

夕やみのロサンゼルスと、（右）　ロサンゼルス国際空港のシンボル、回転レストランの建物。